WELCOME TO SPEEDWAY

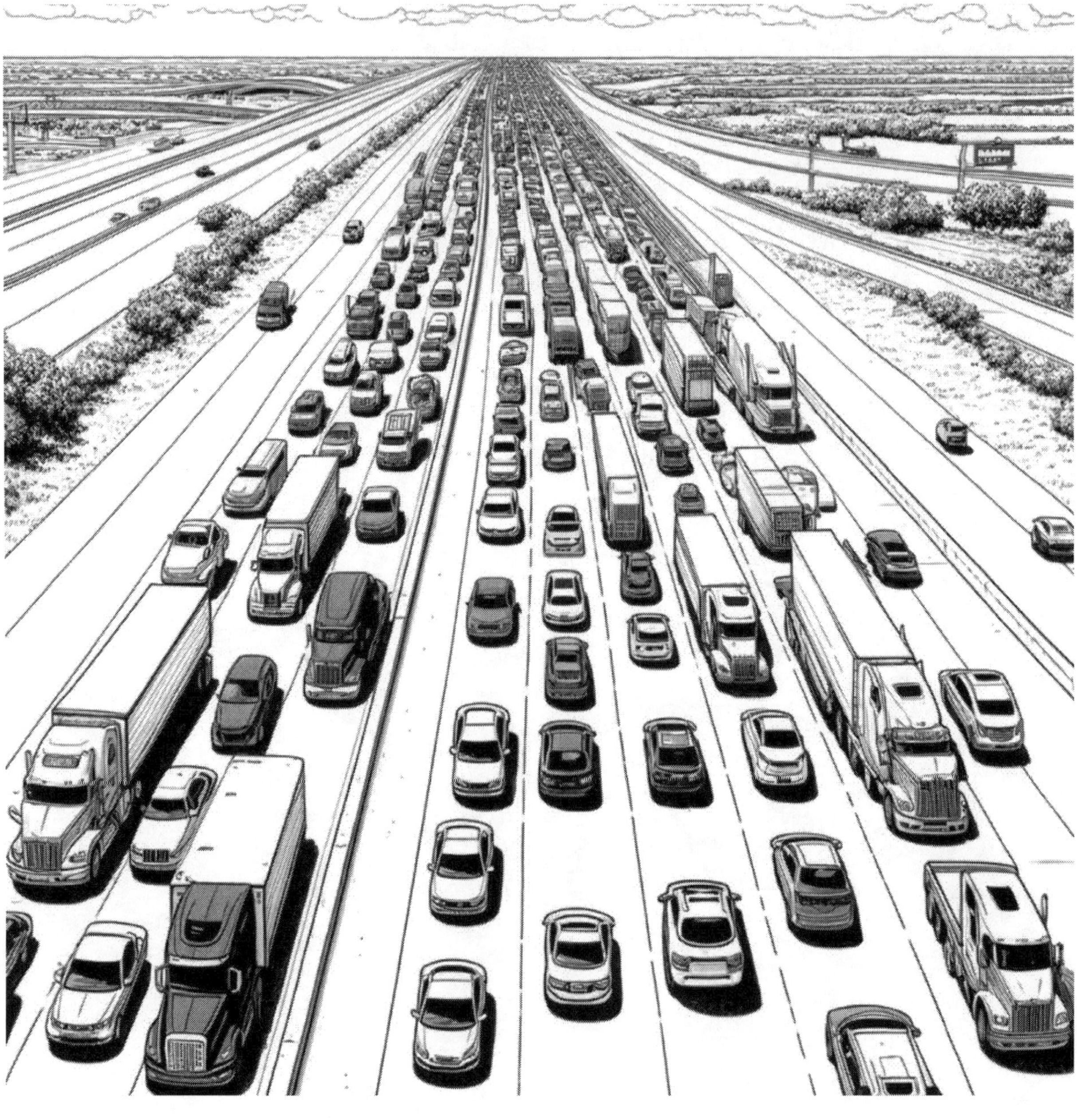

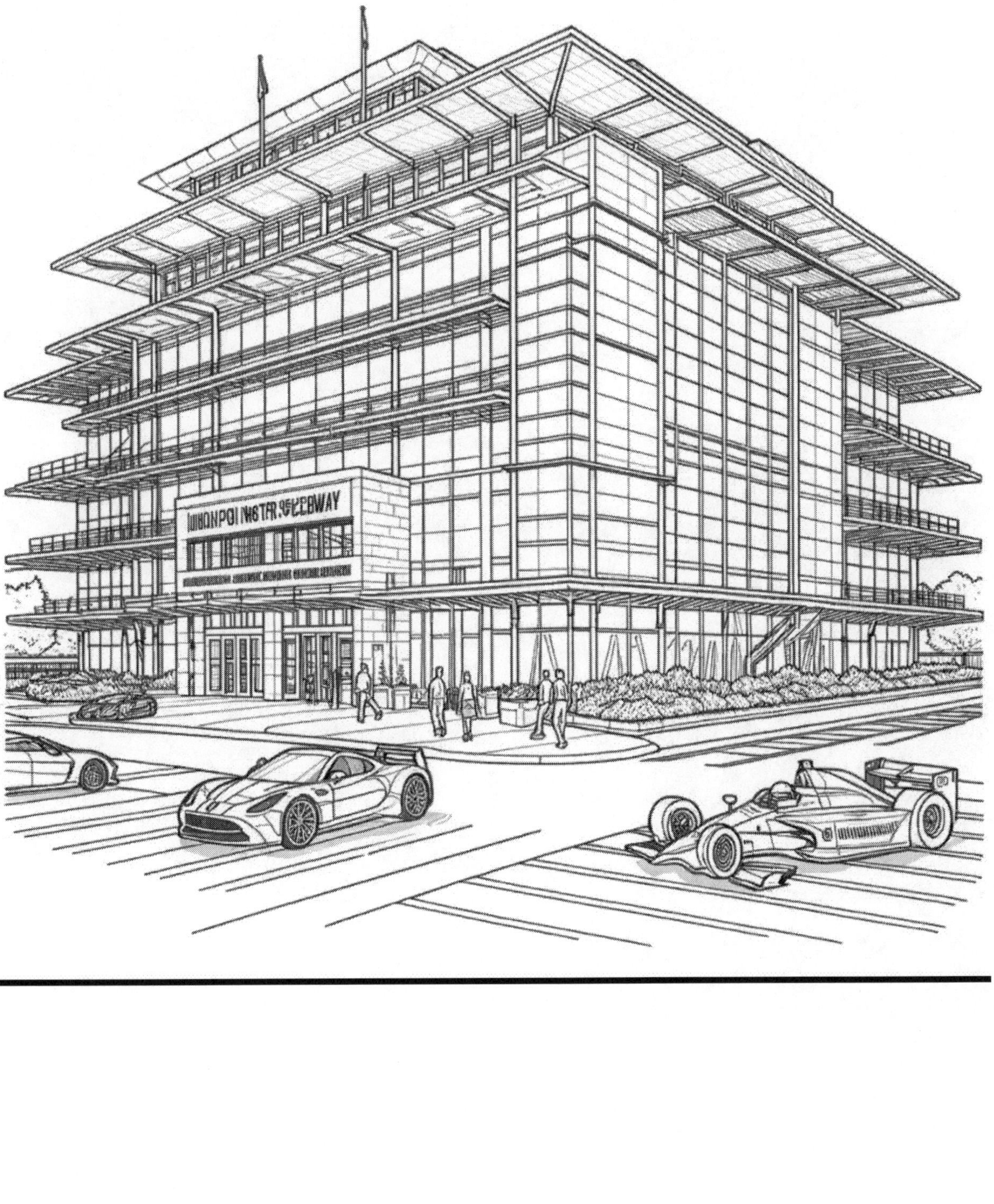

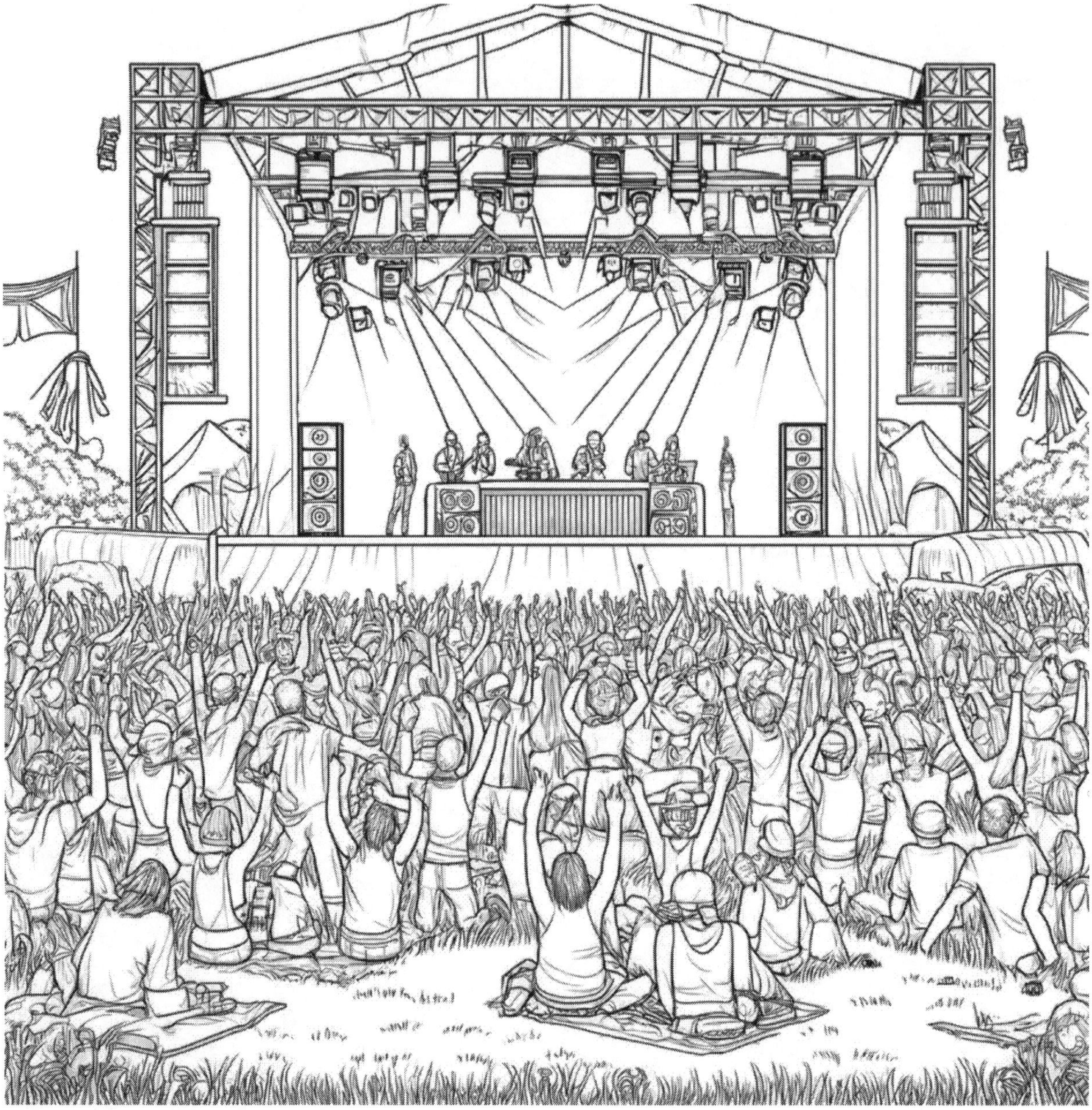

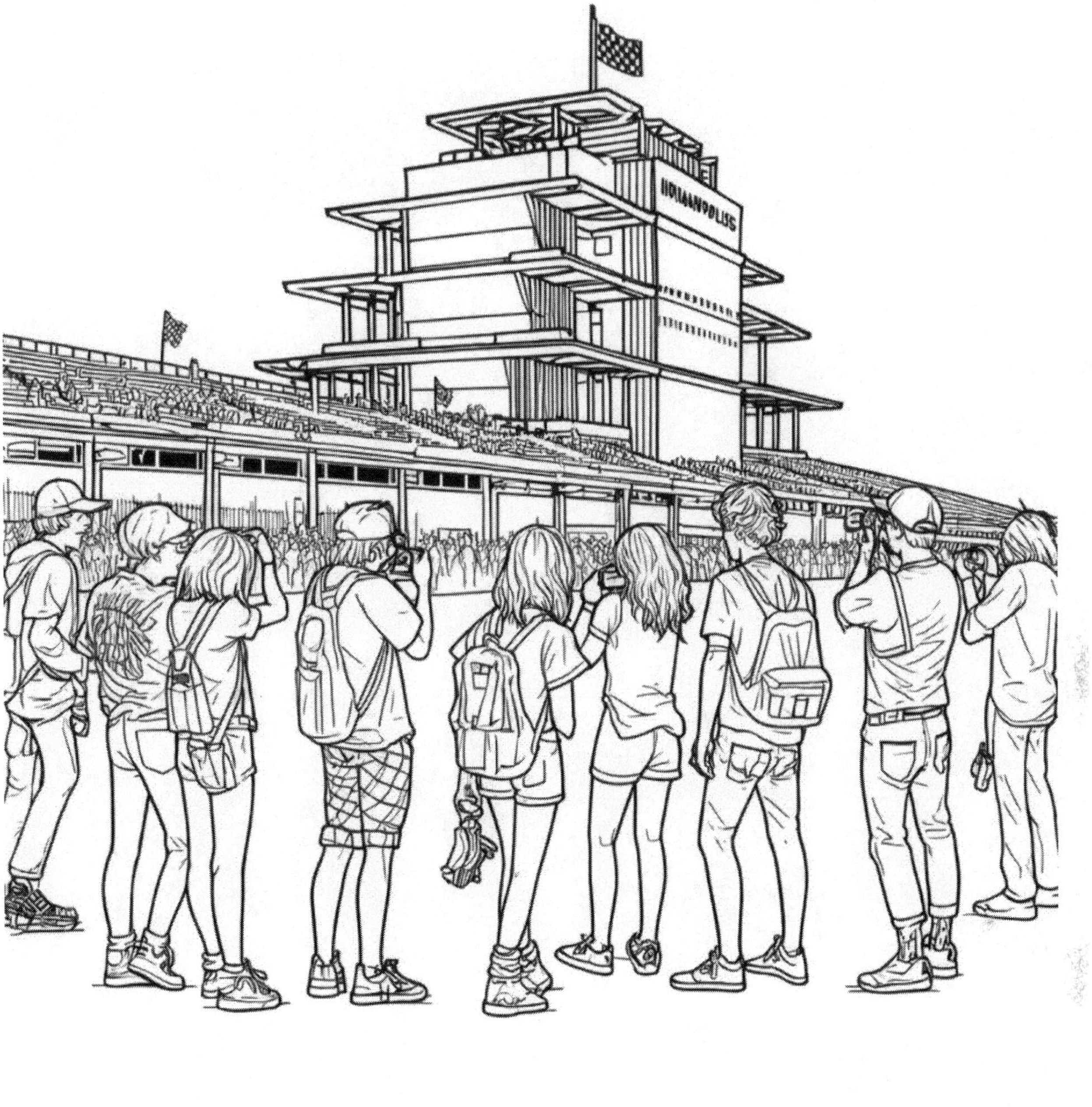

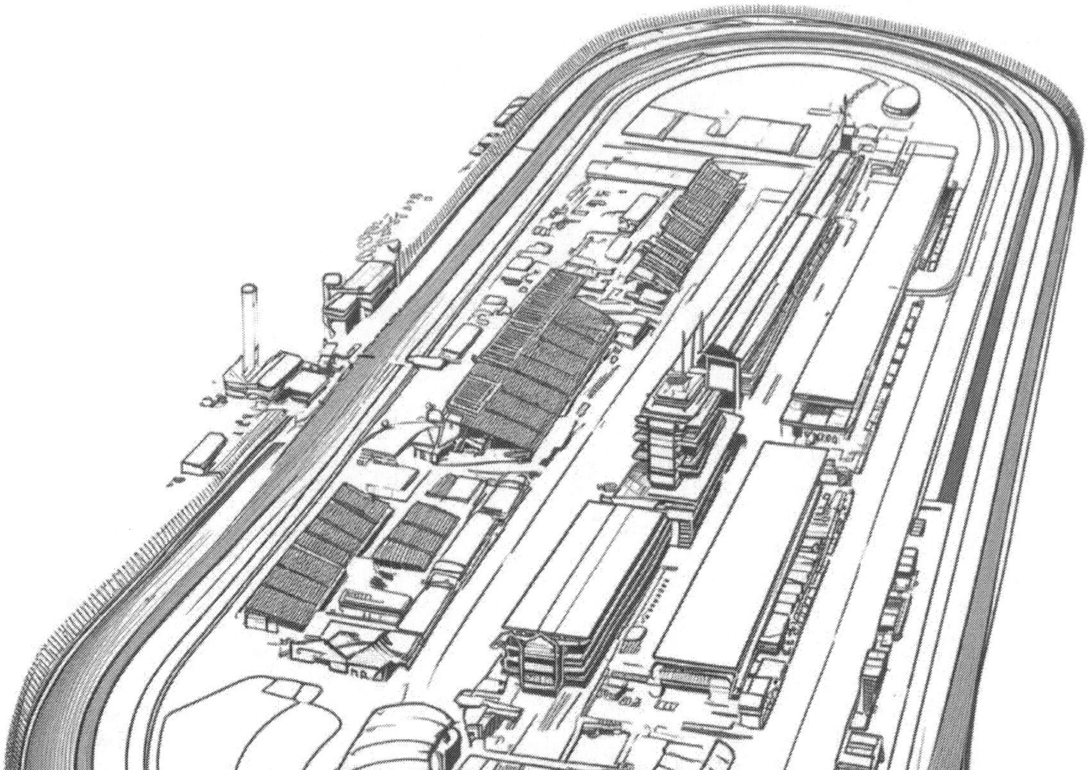

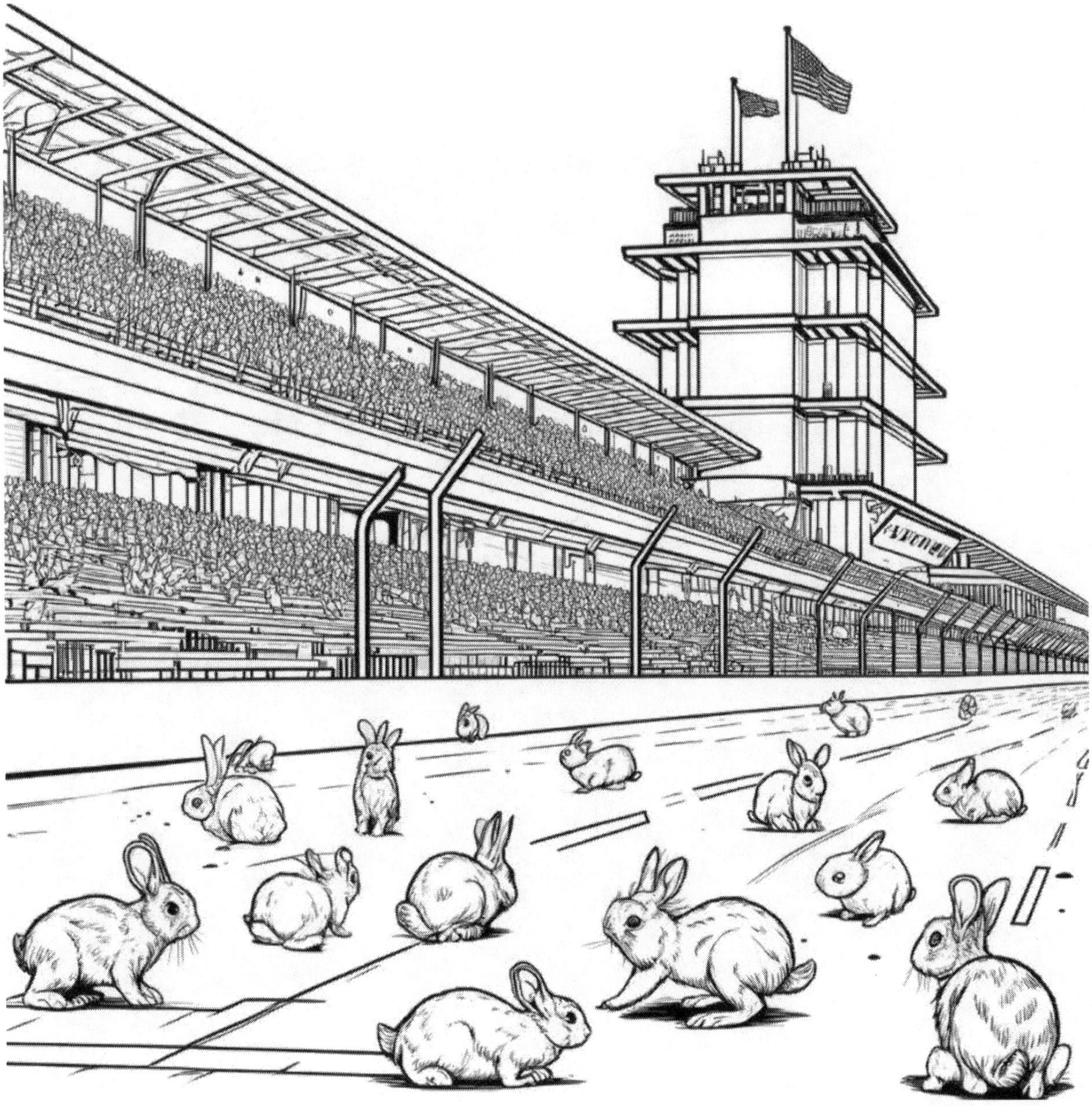

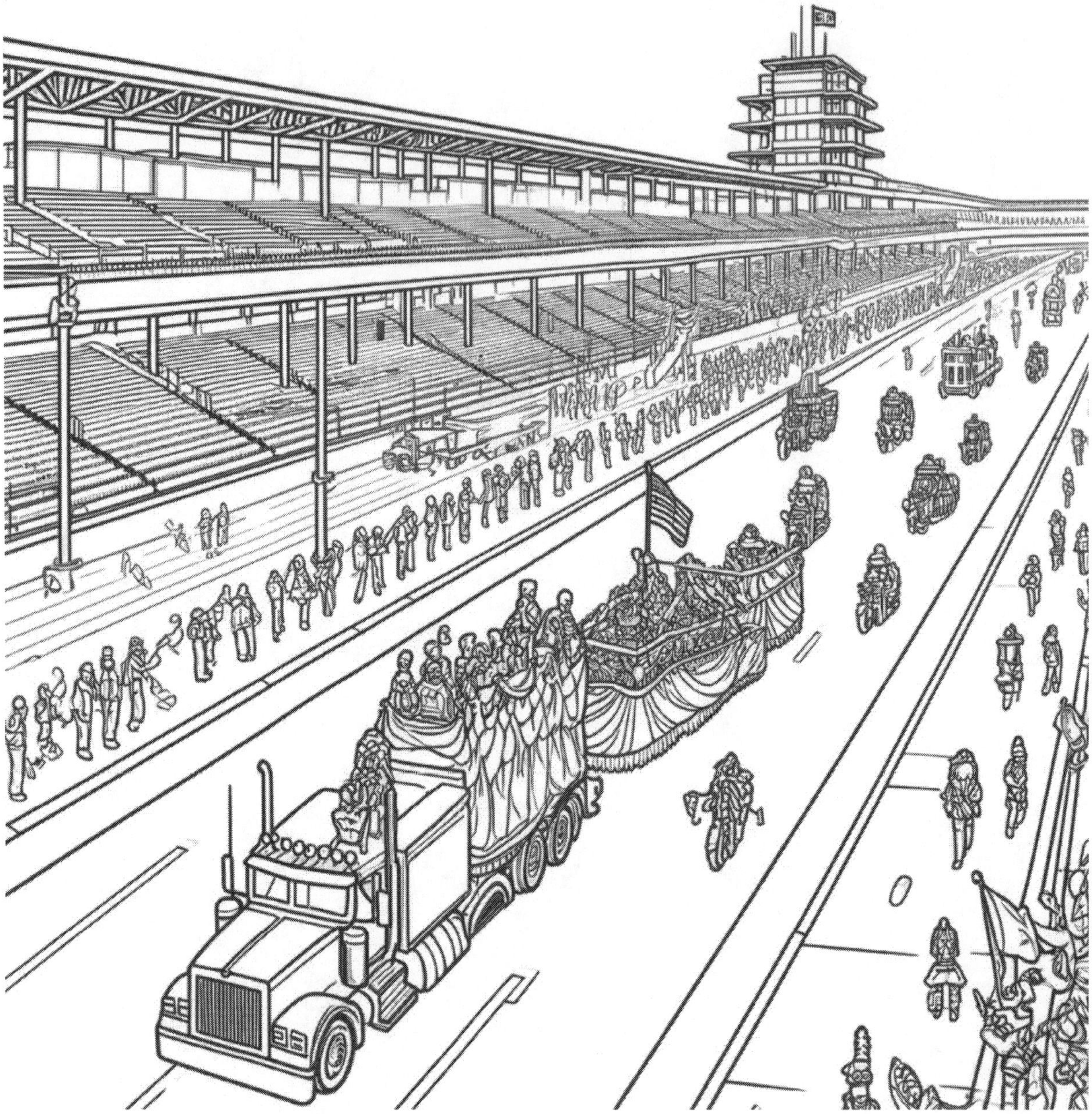

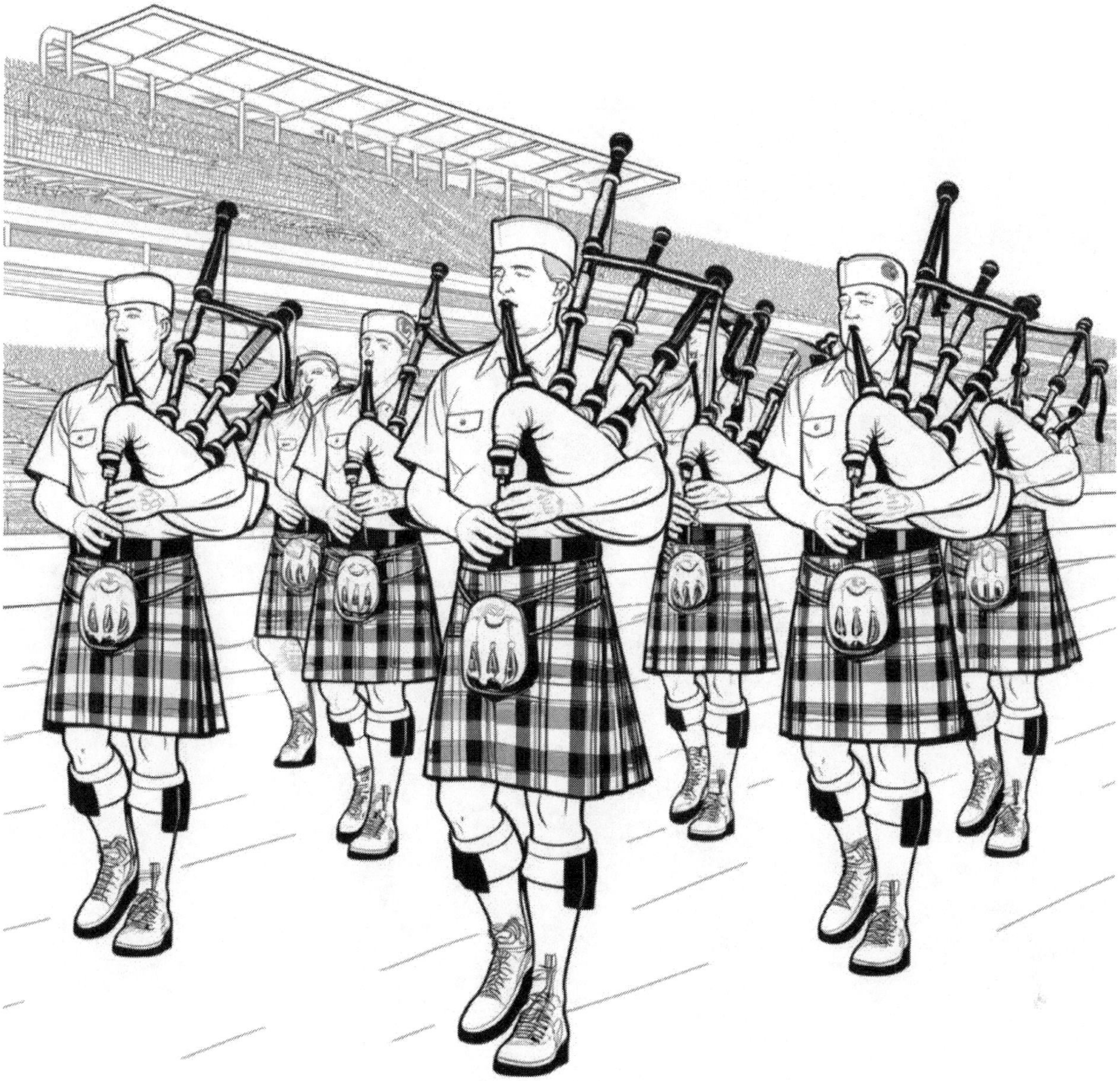

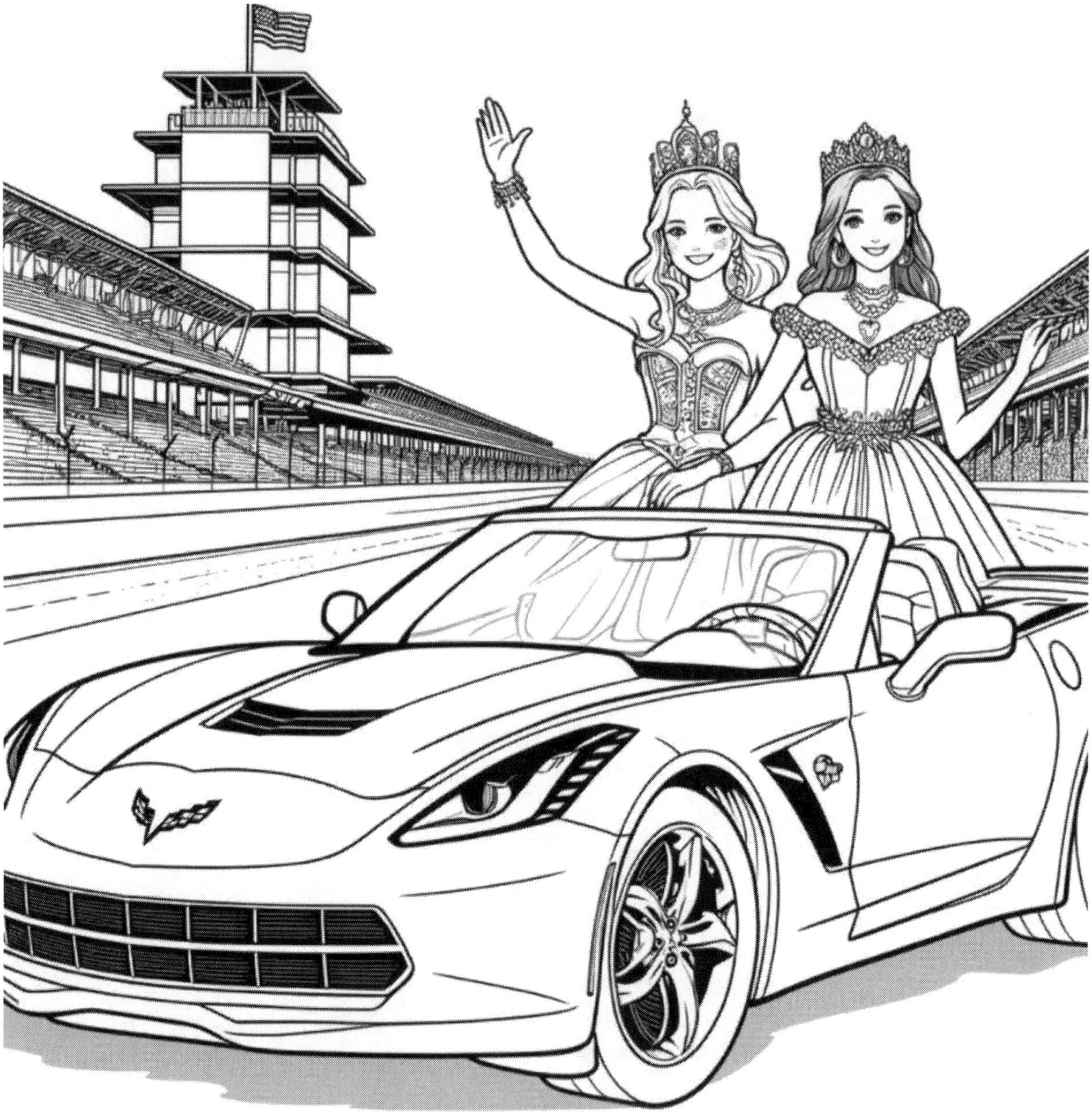

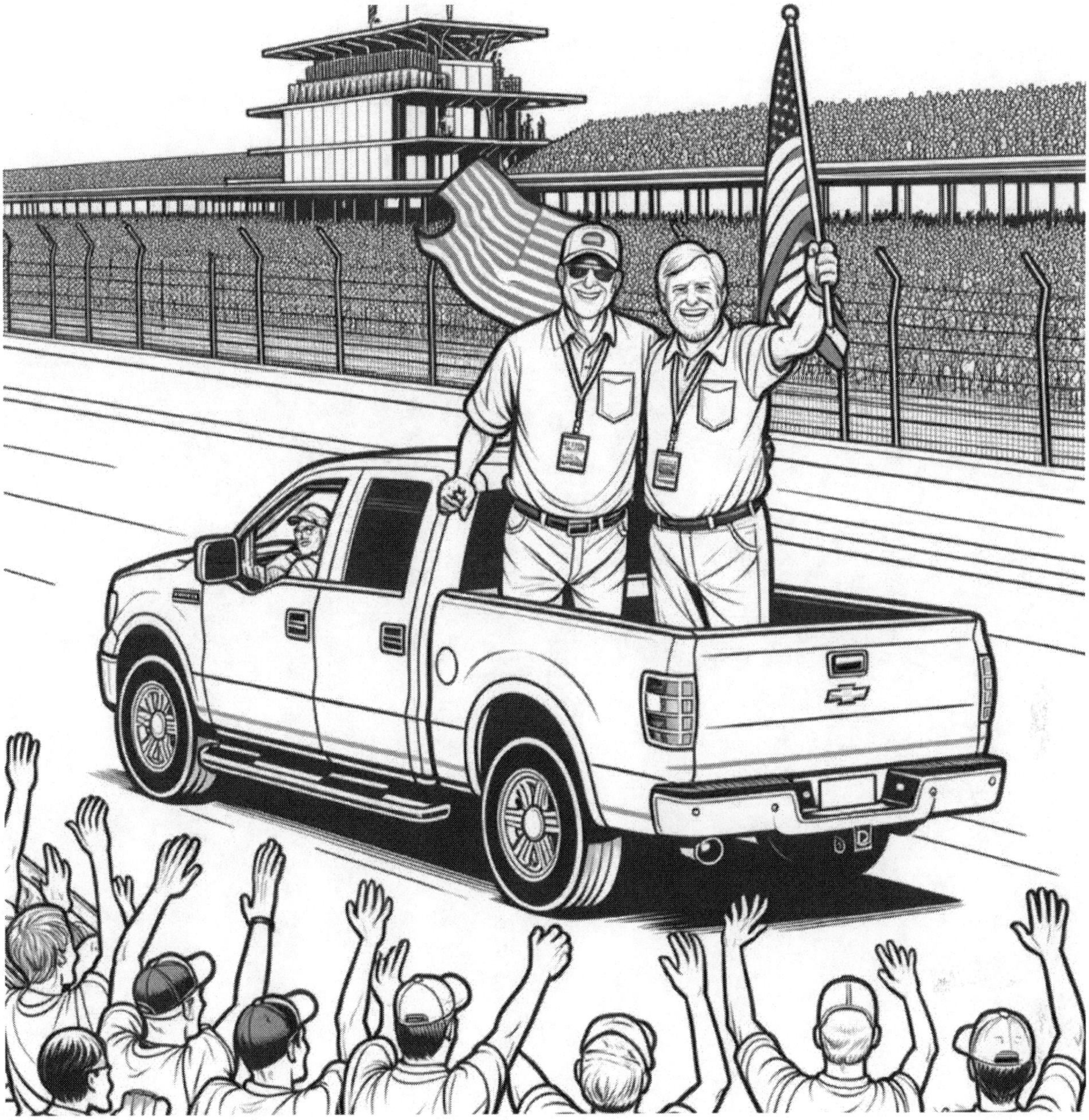

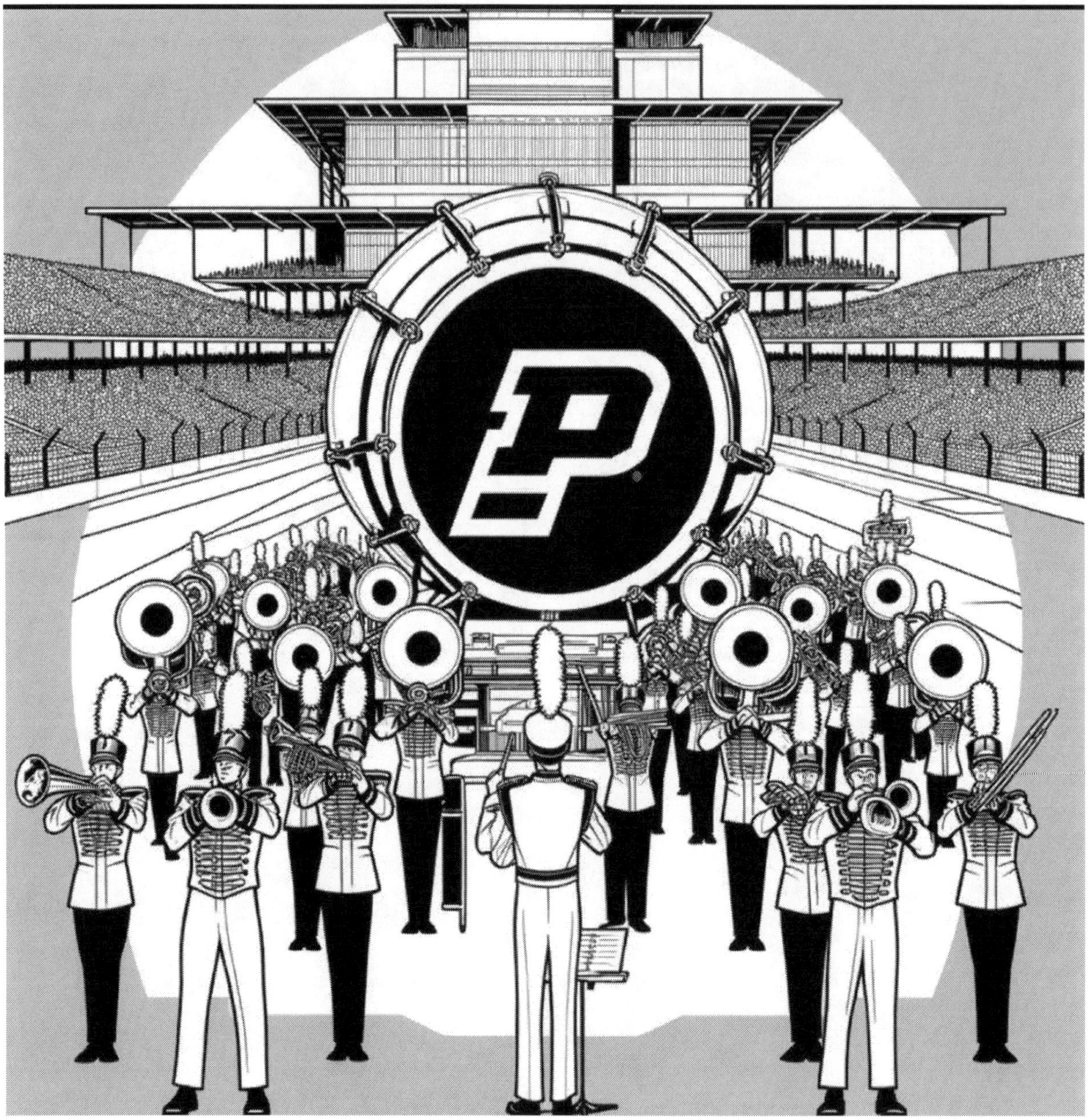

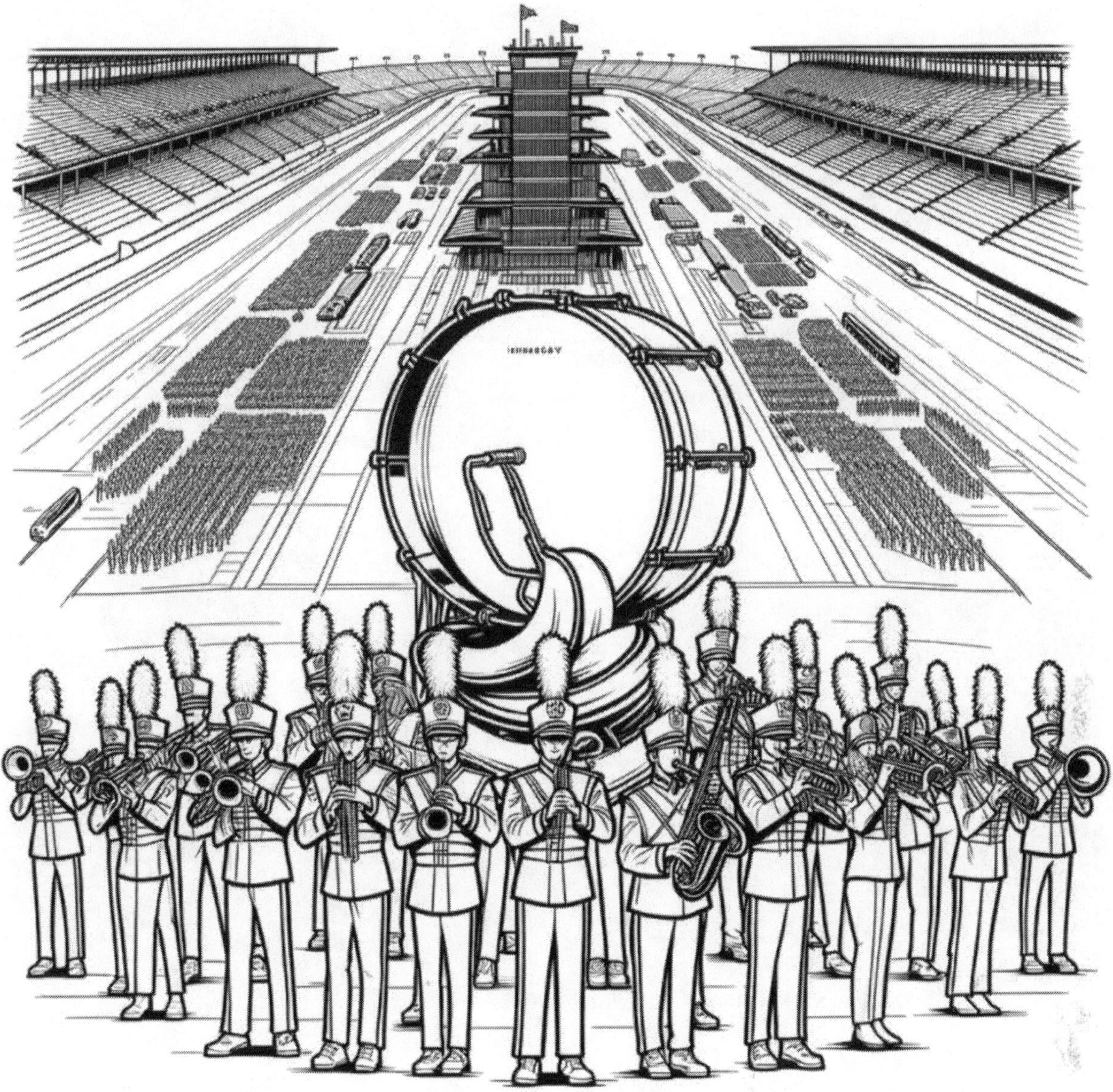

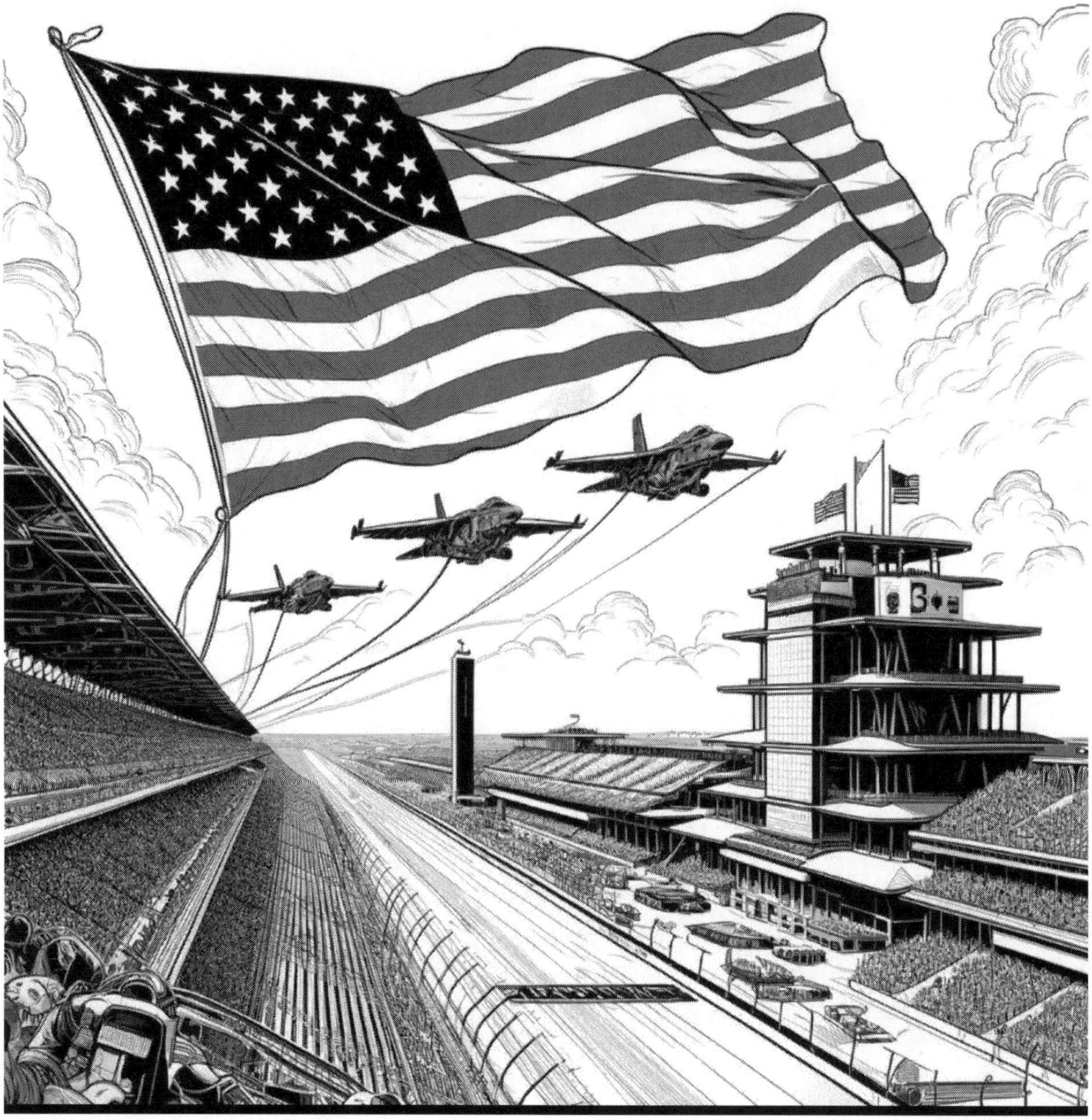

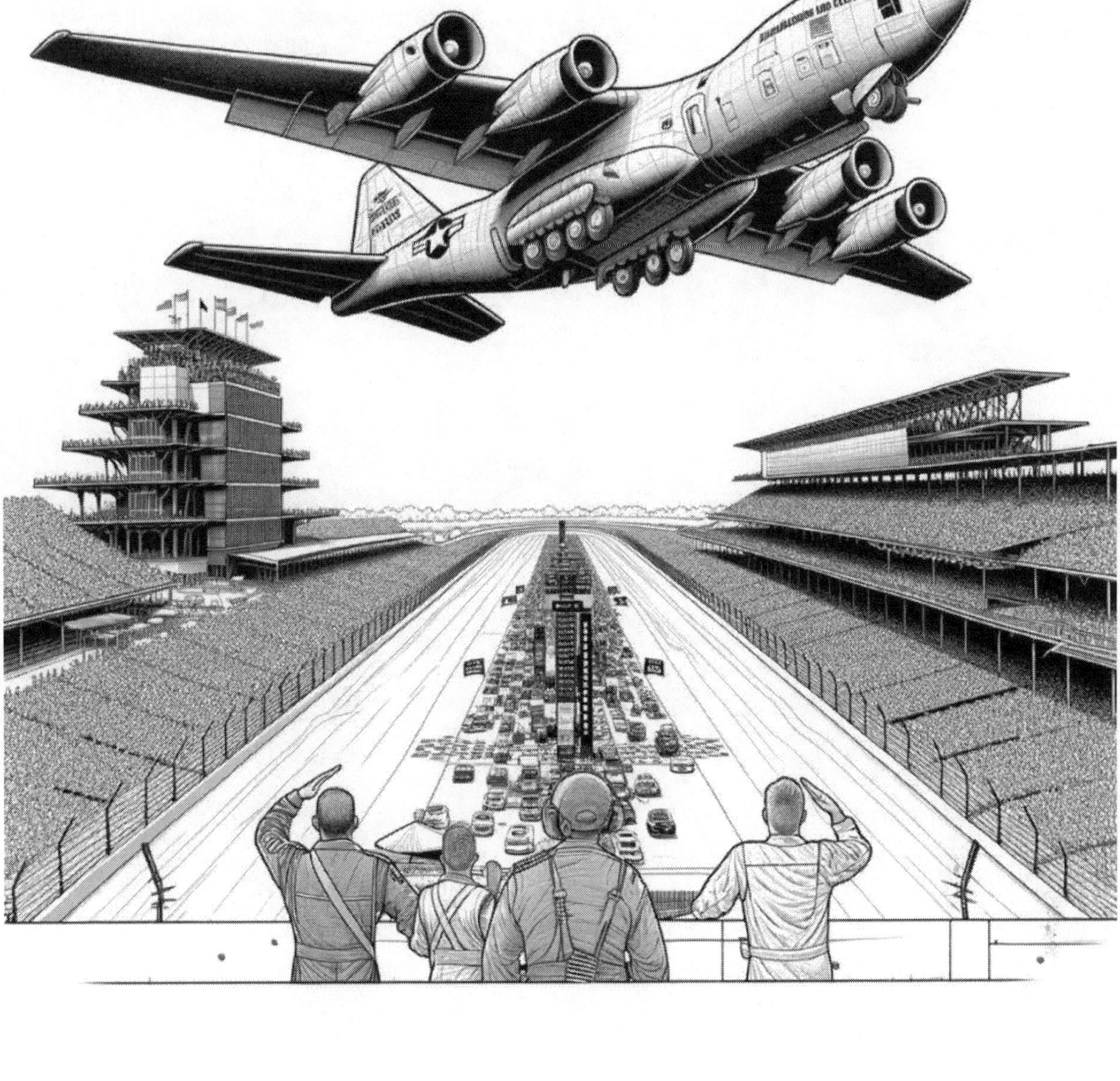

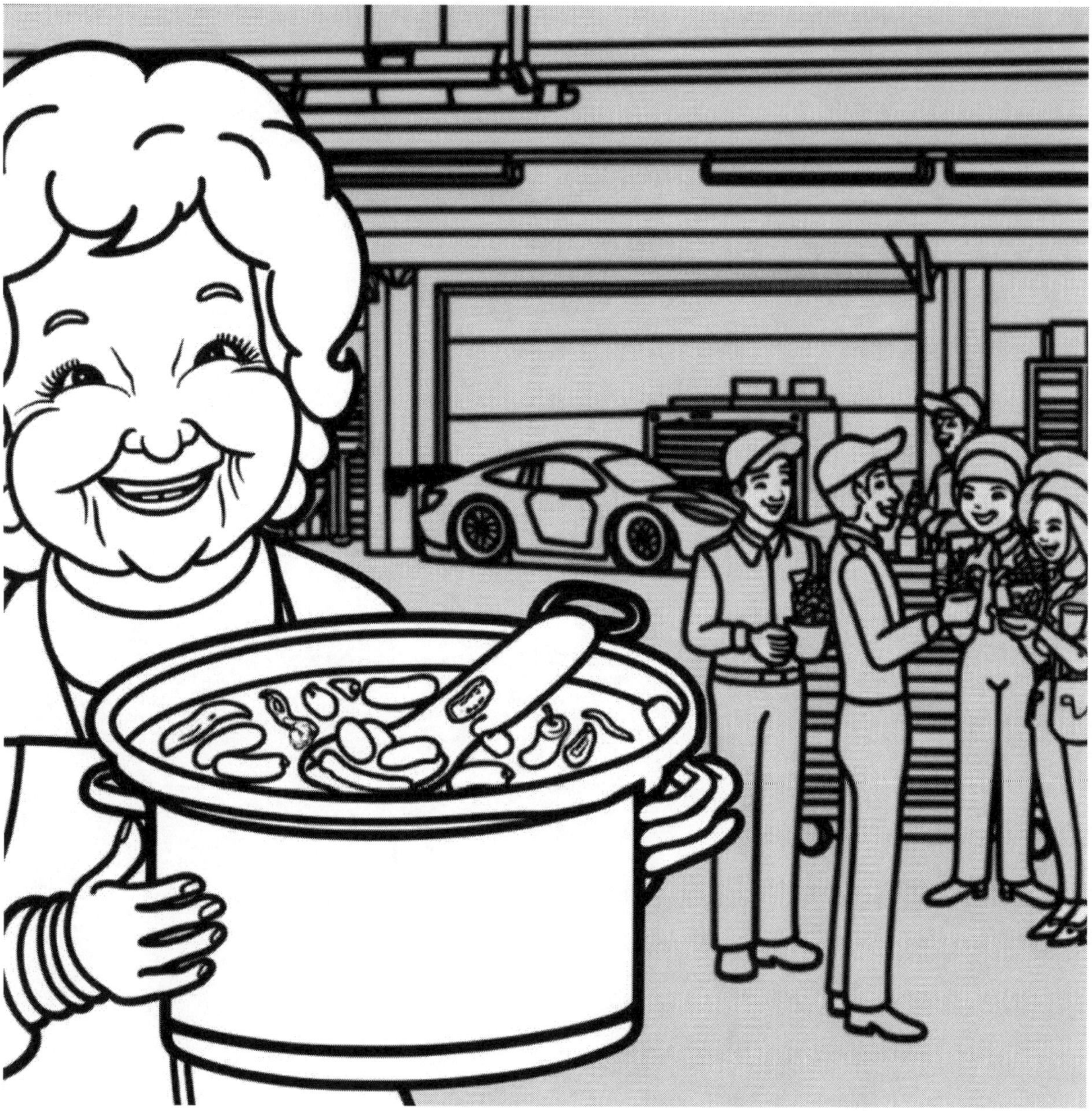

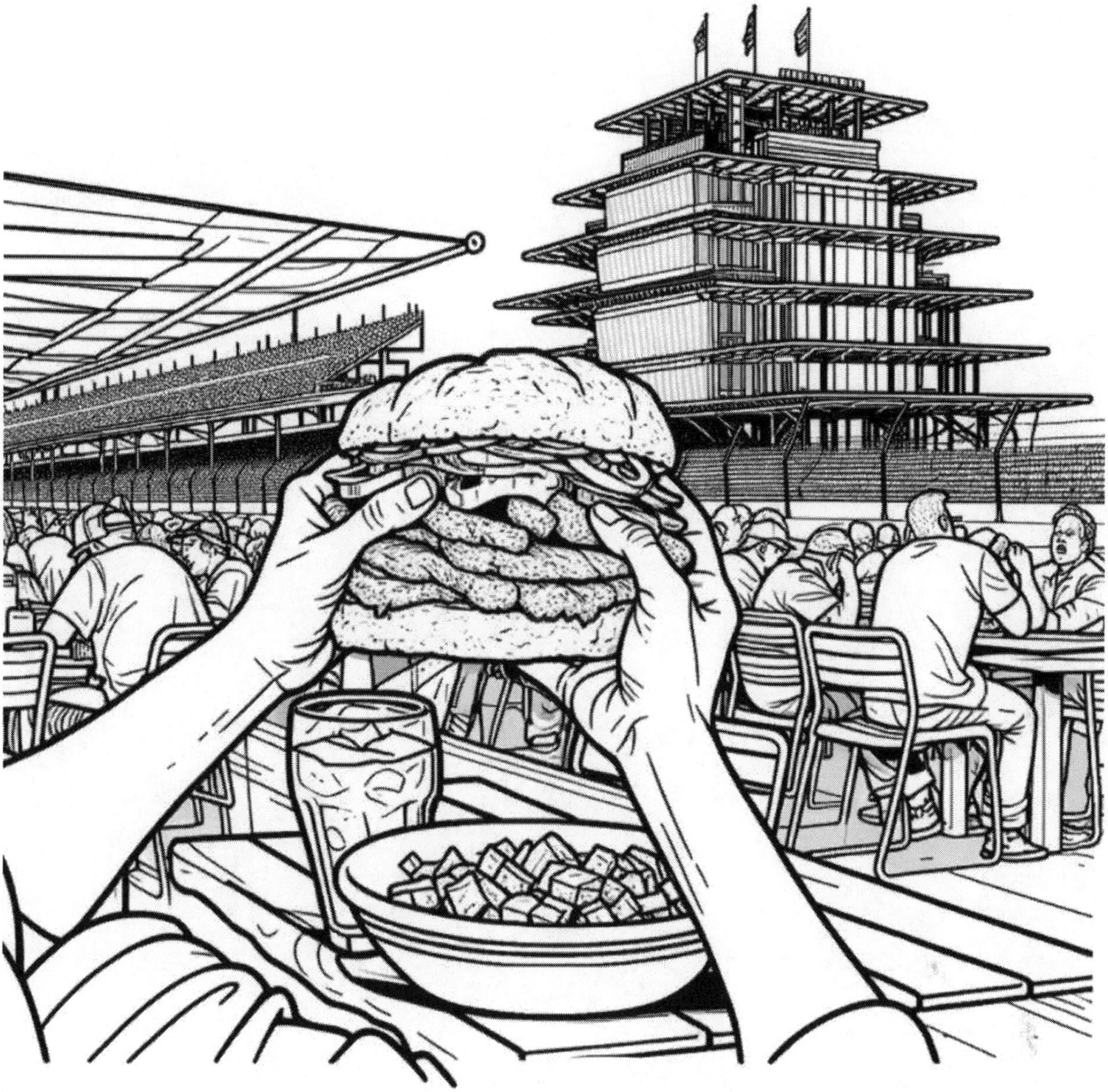

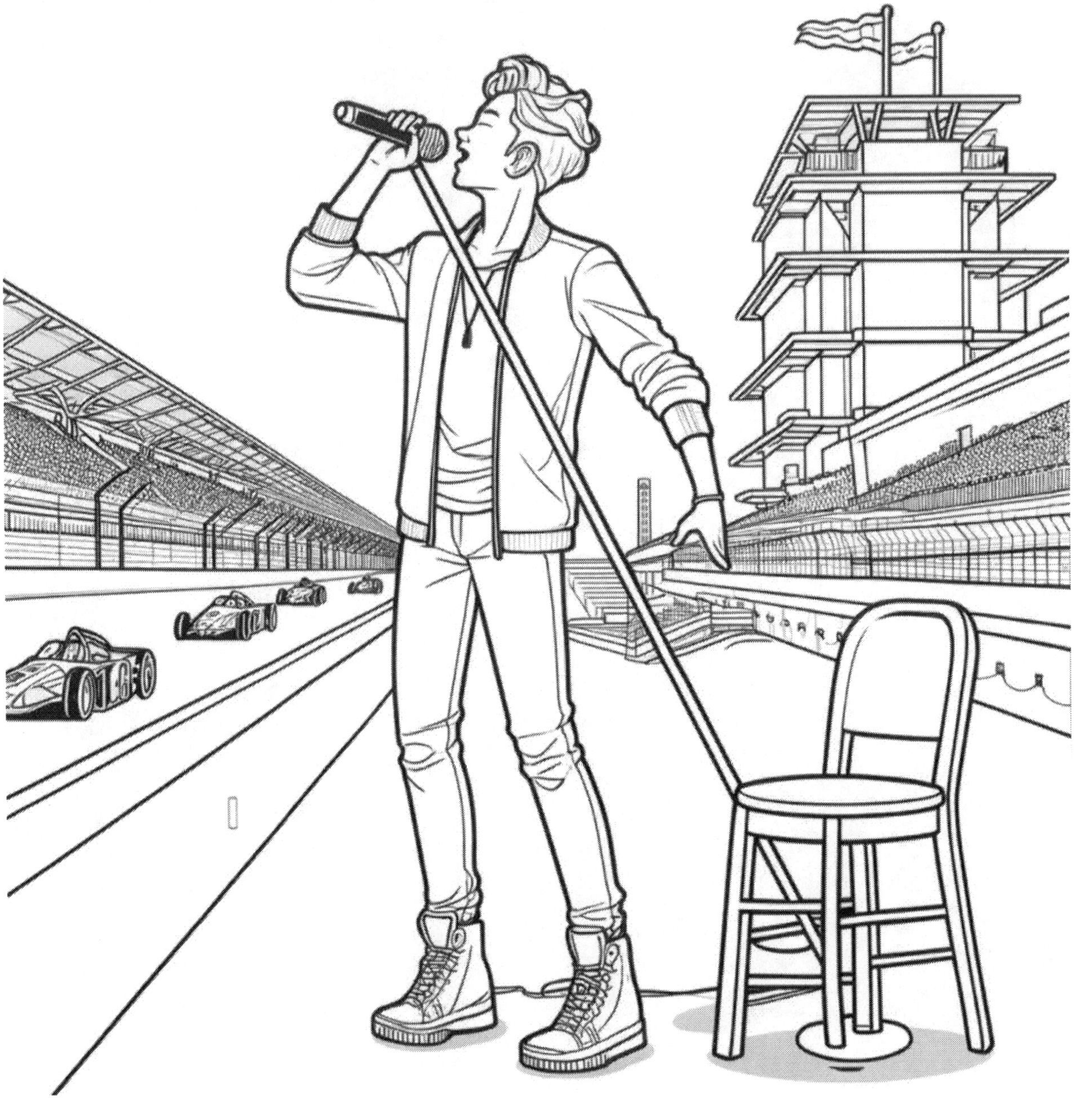

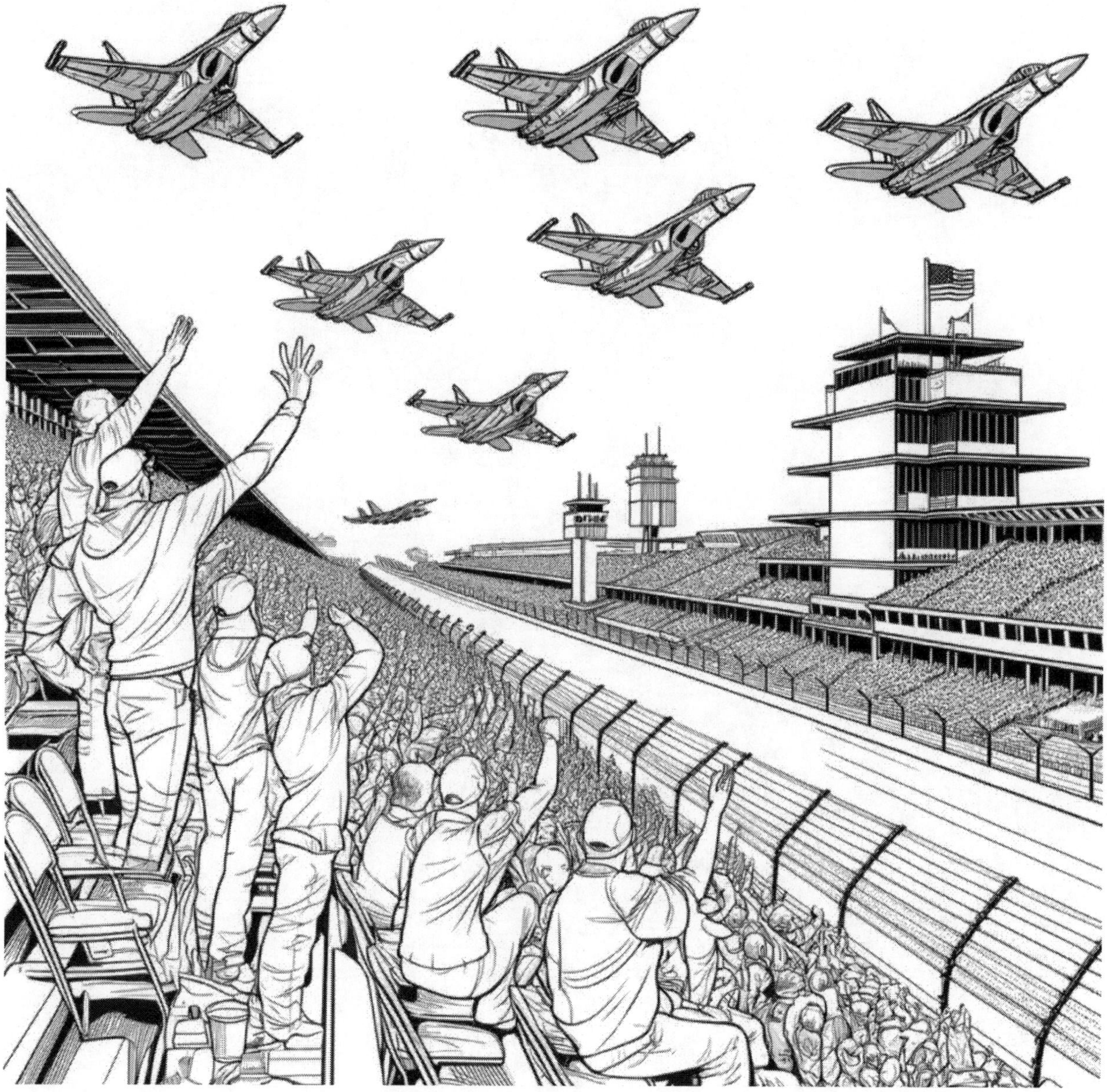

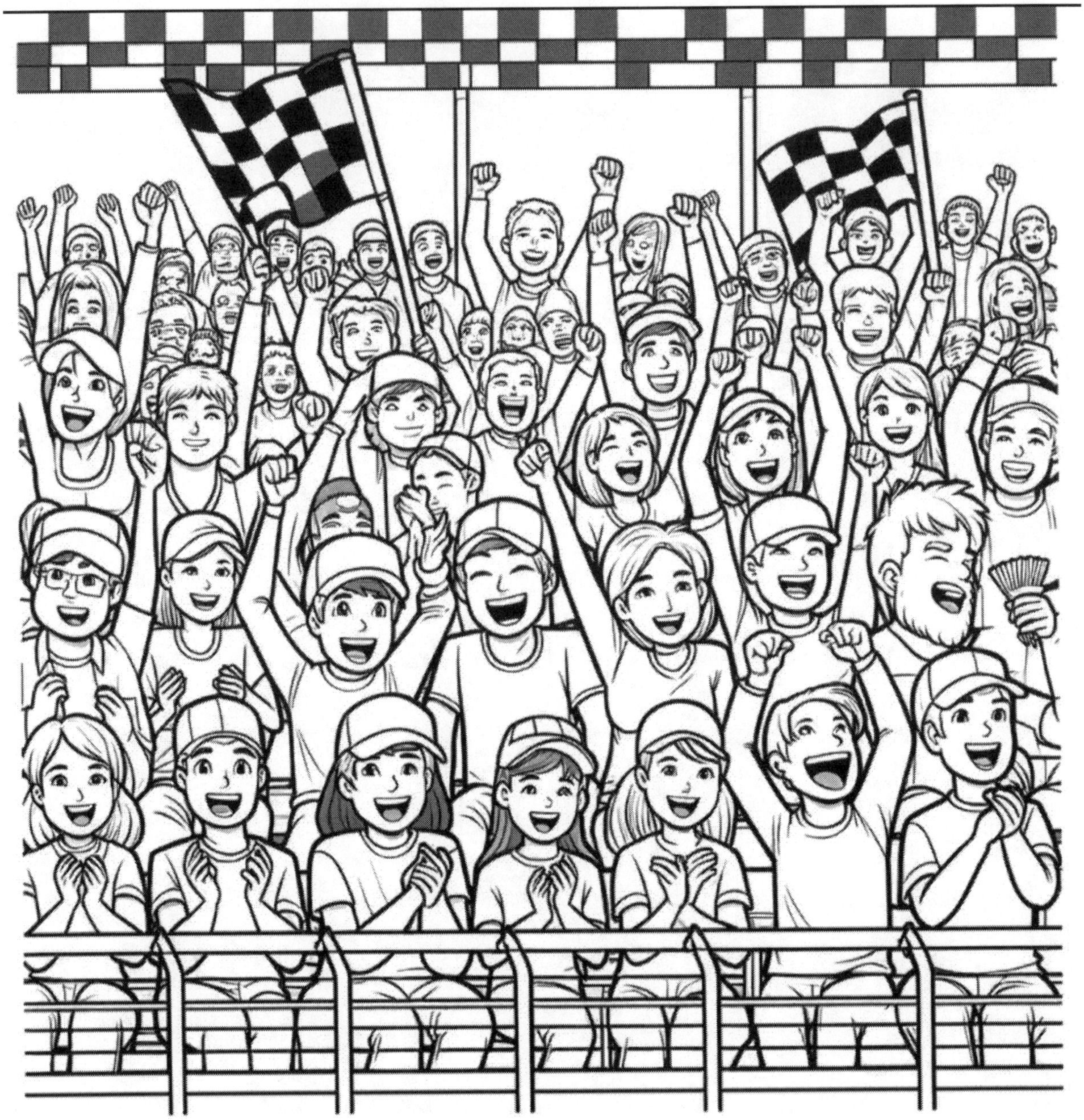

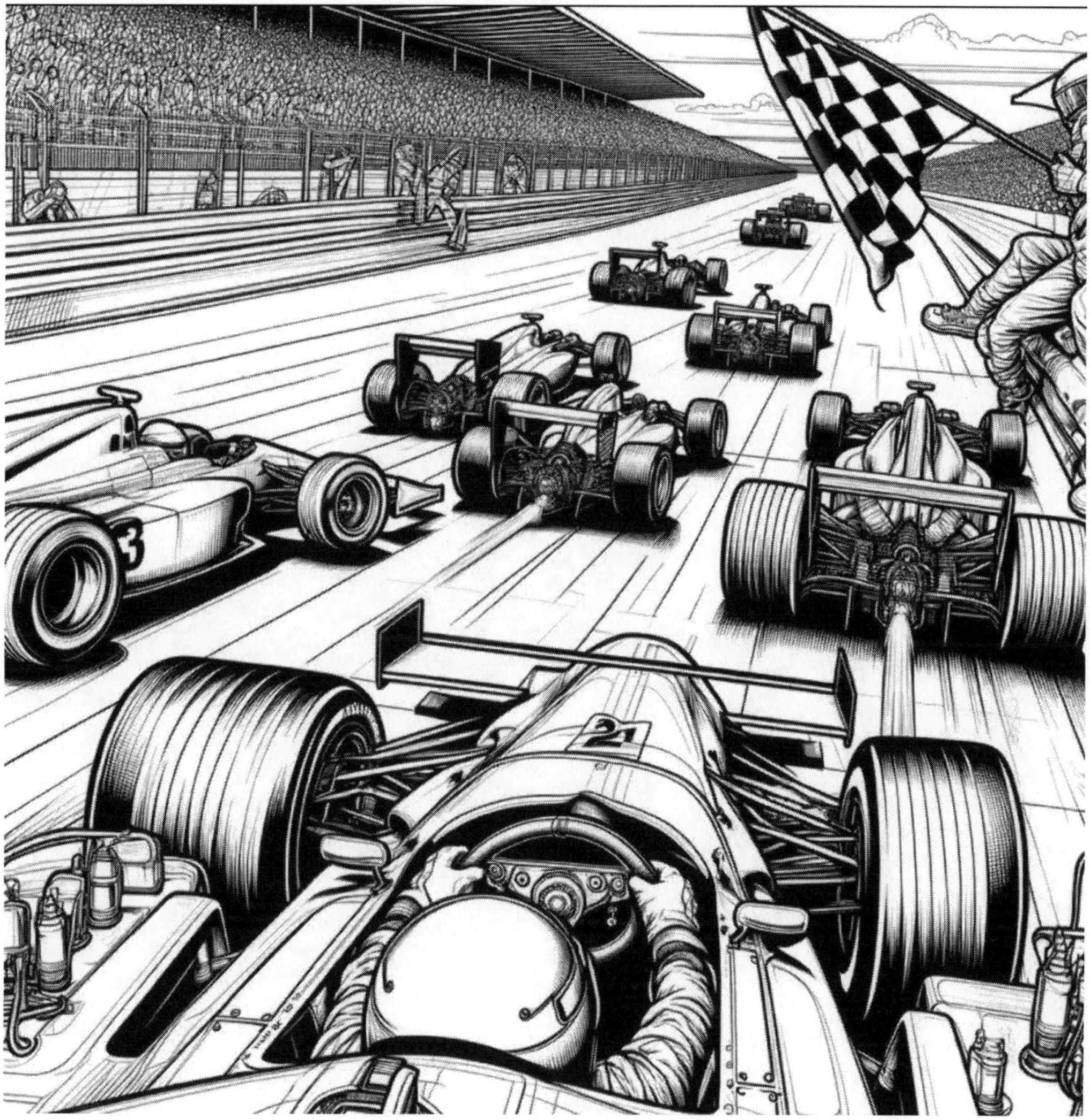

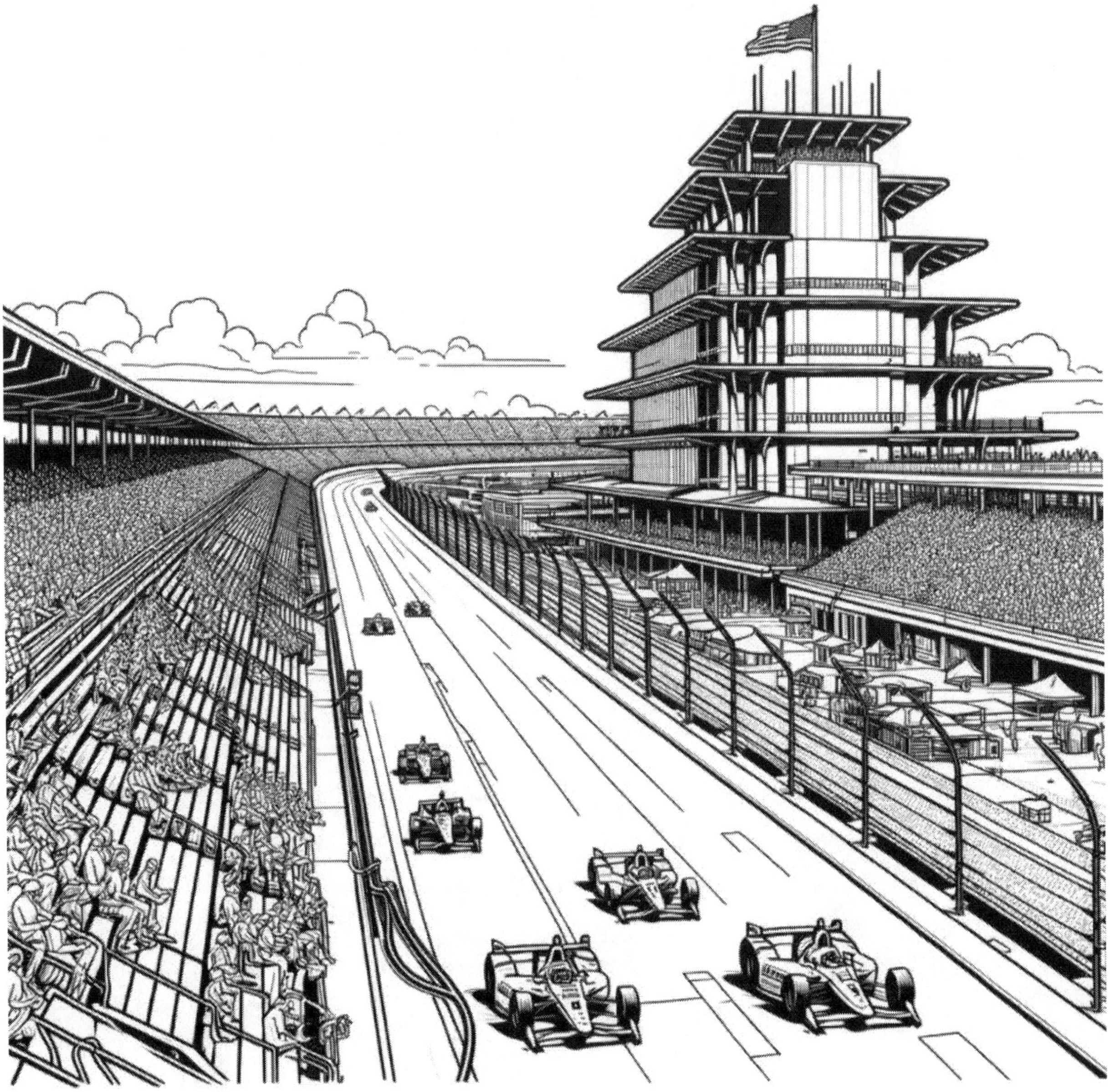

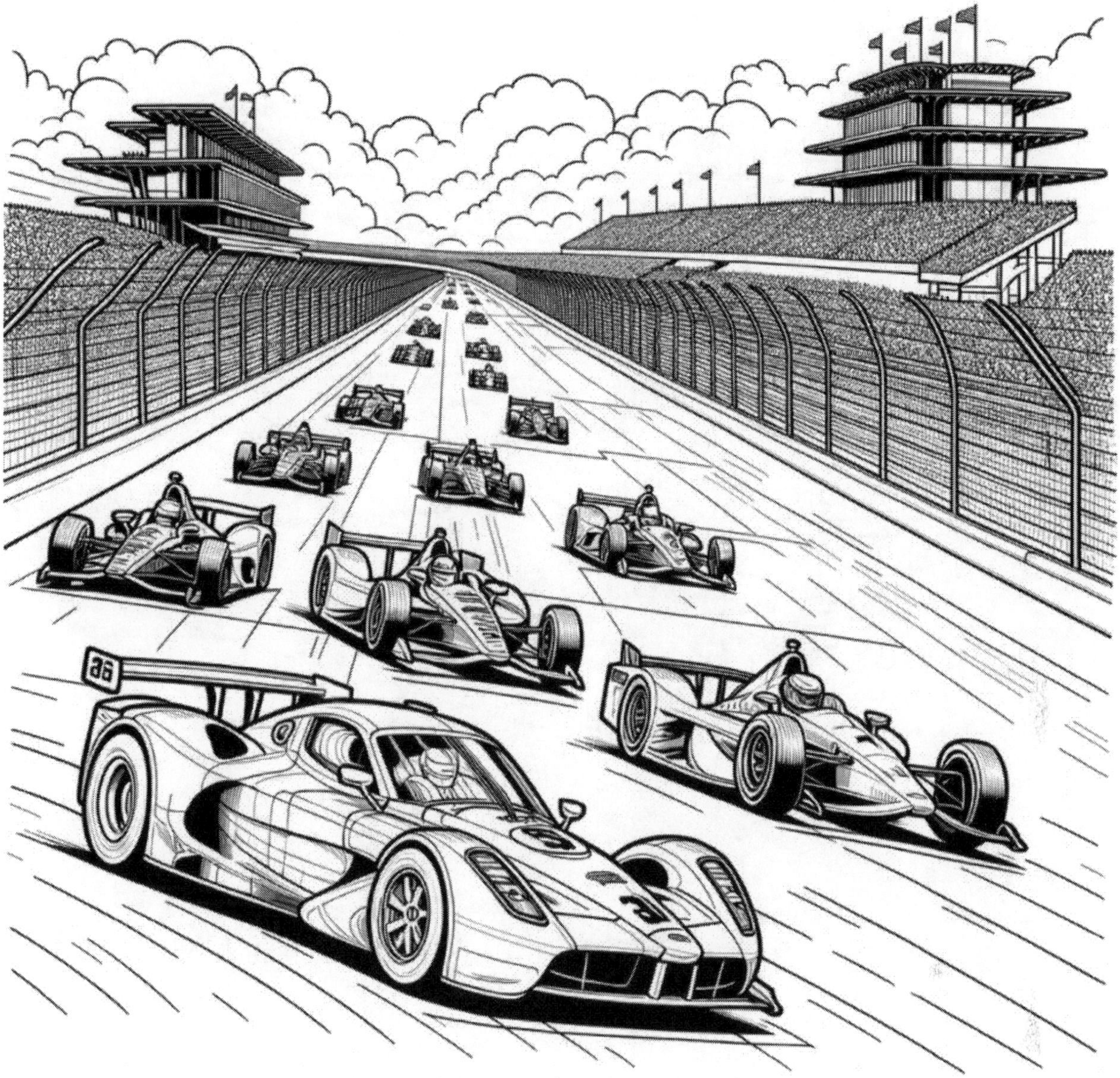

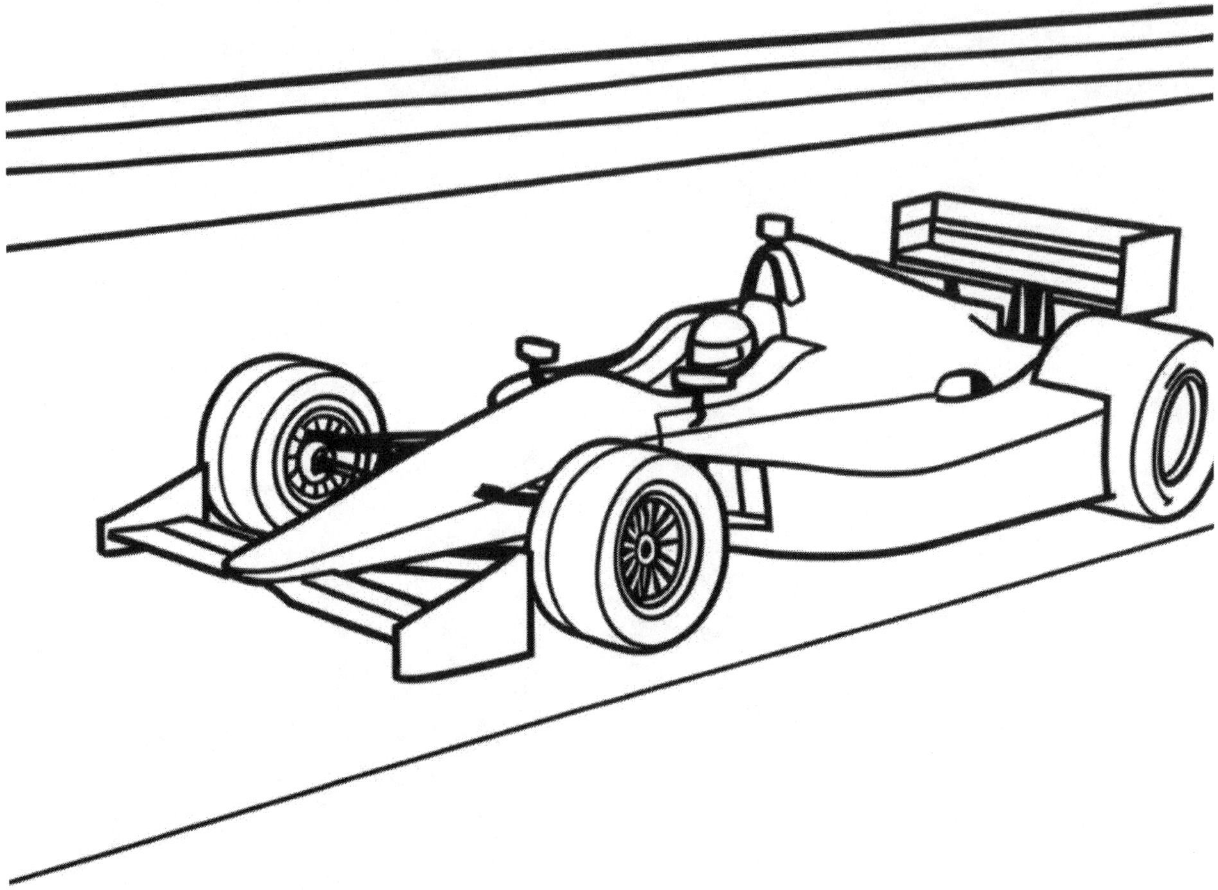

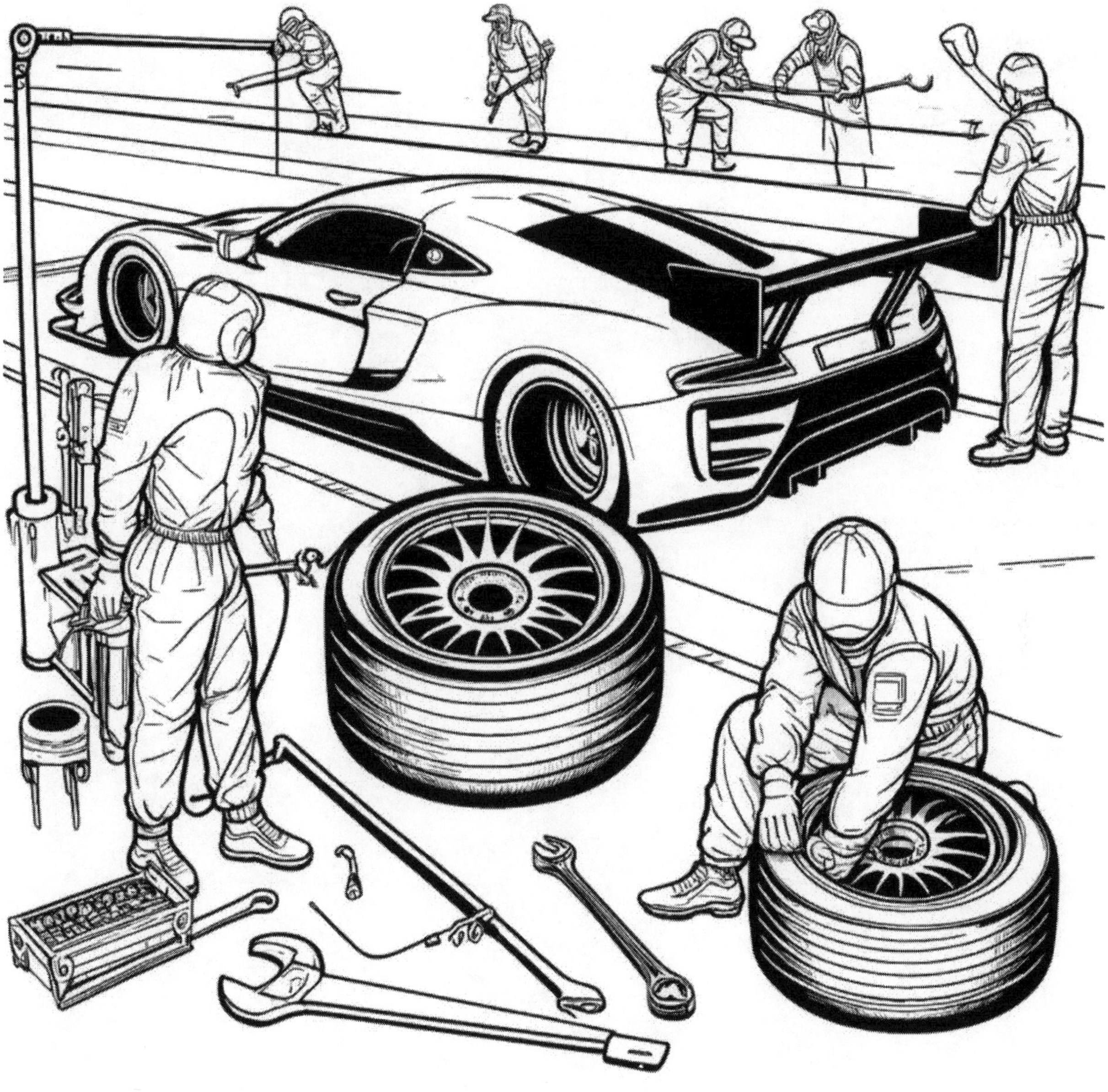

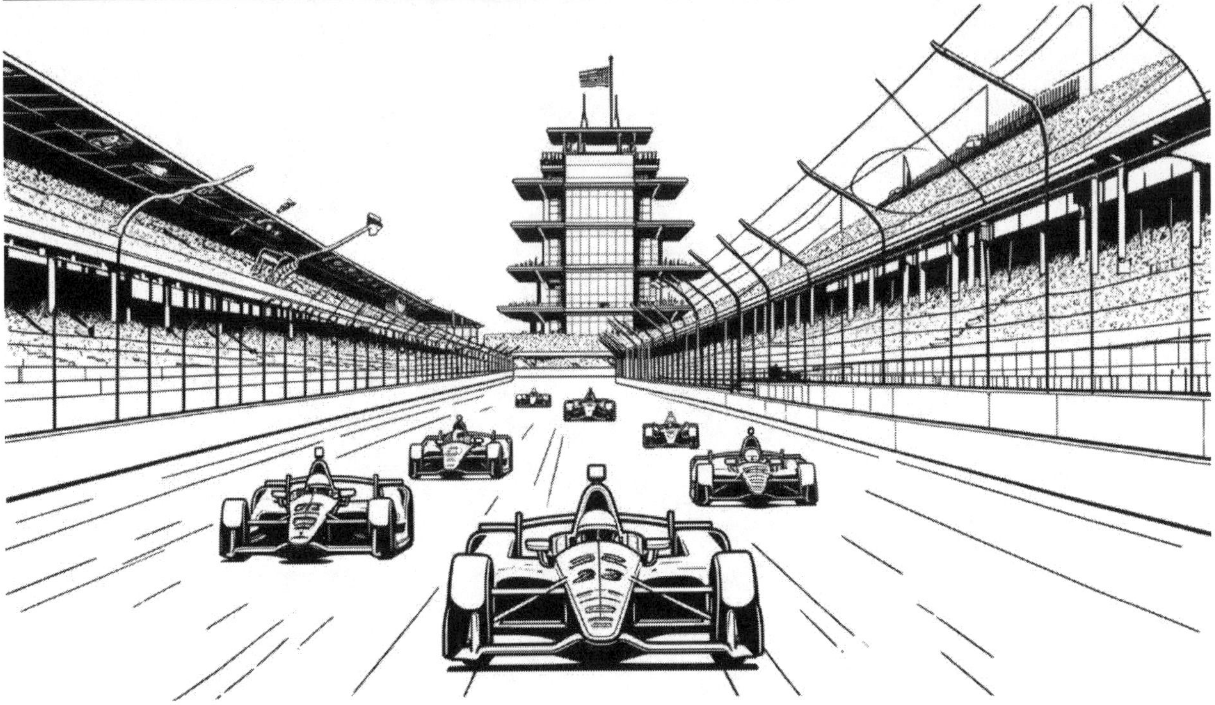

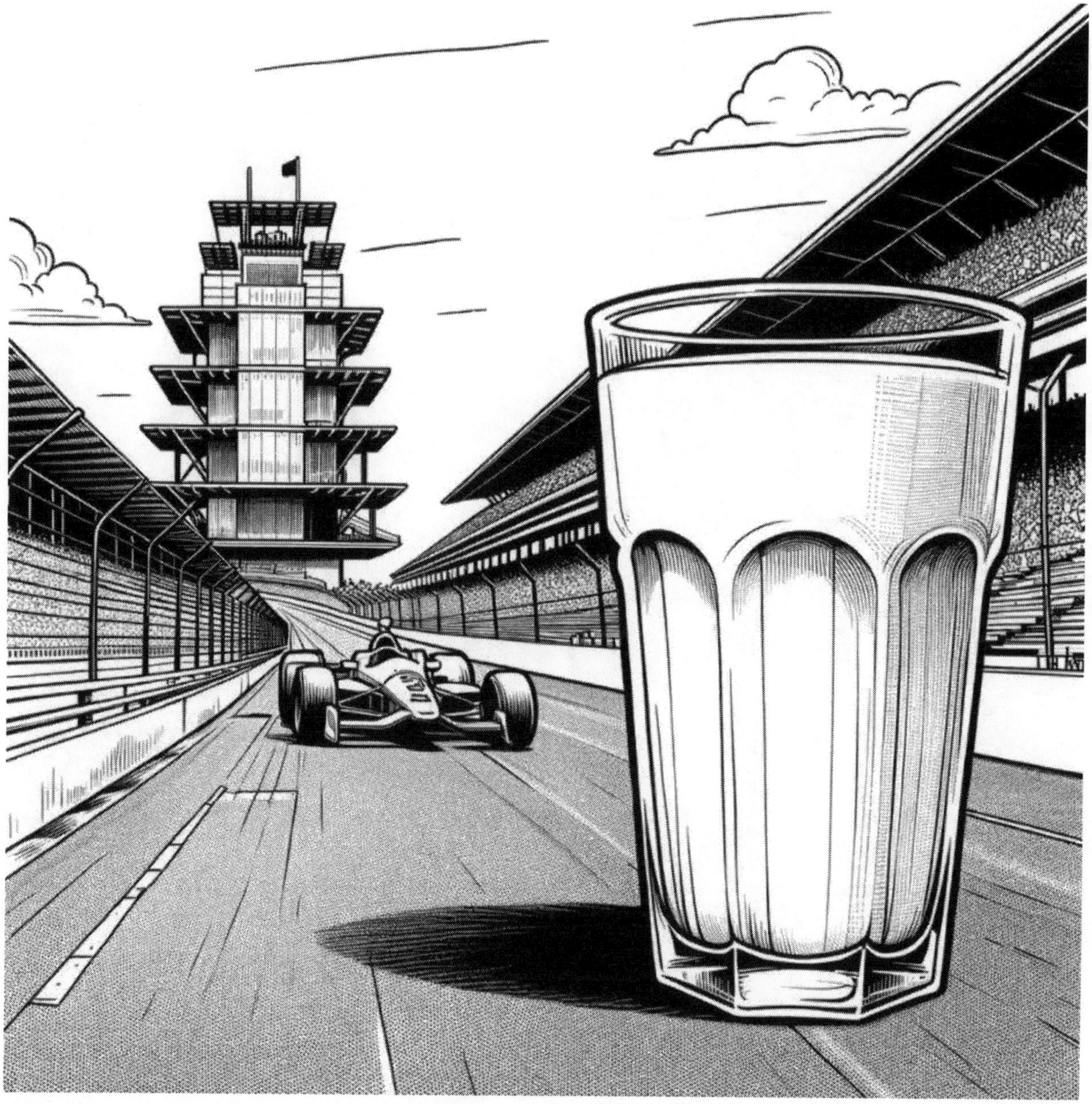

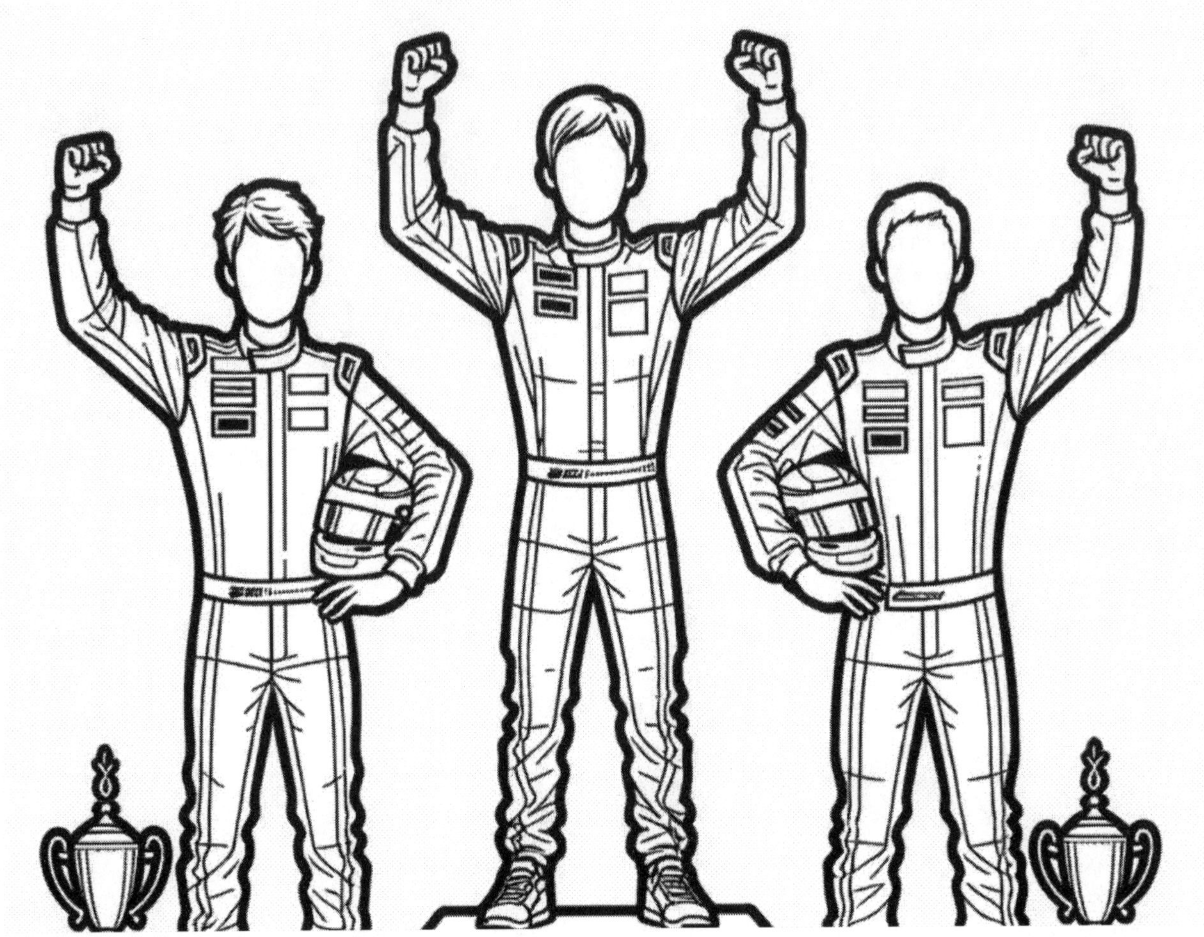

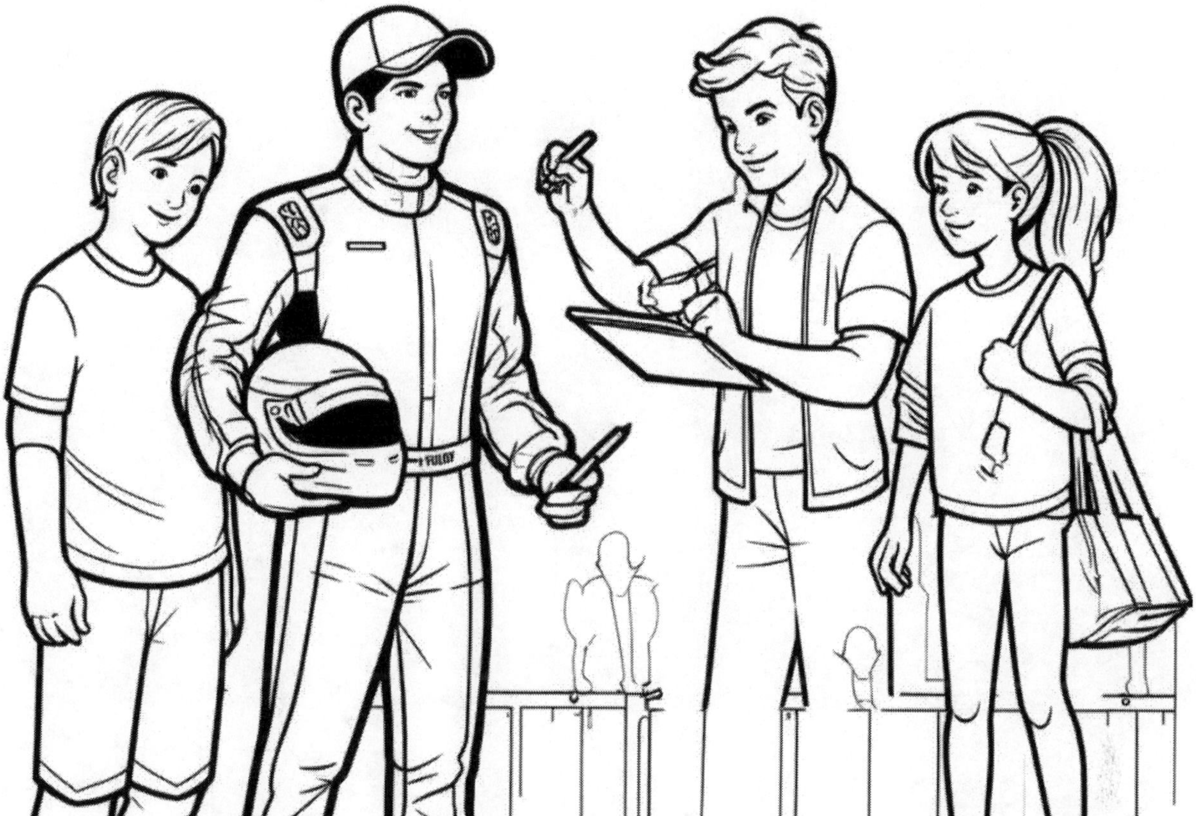

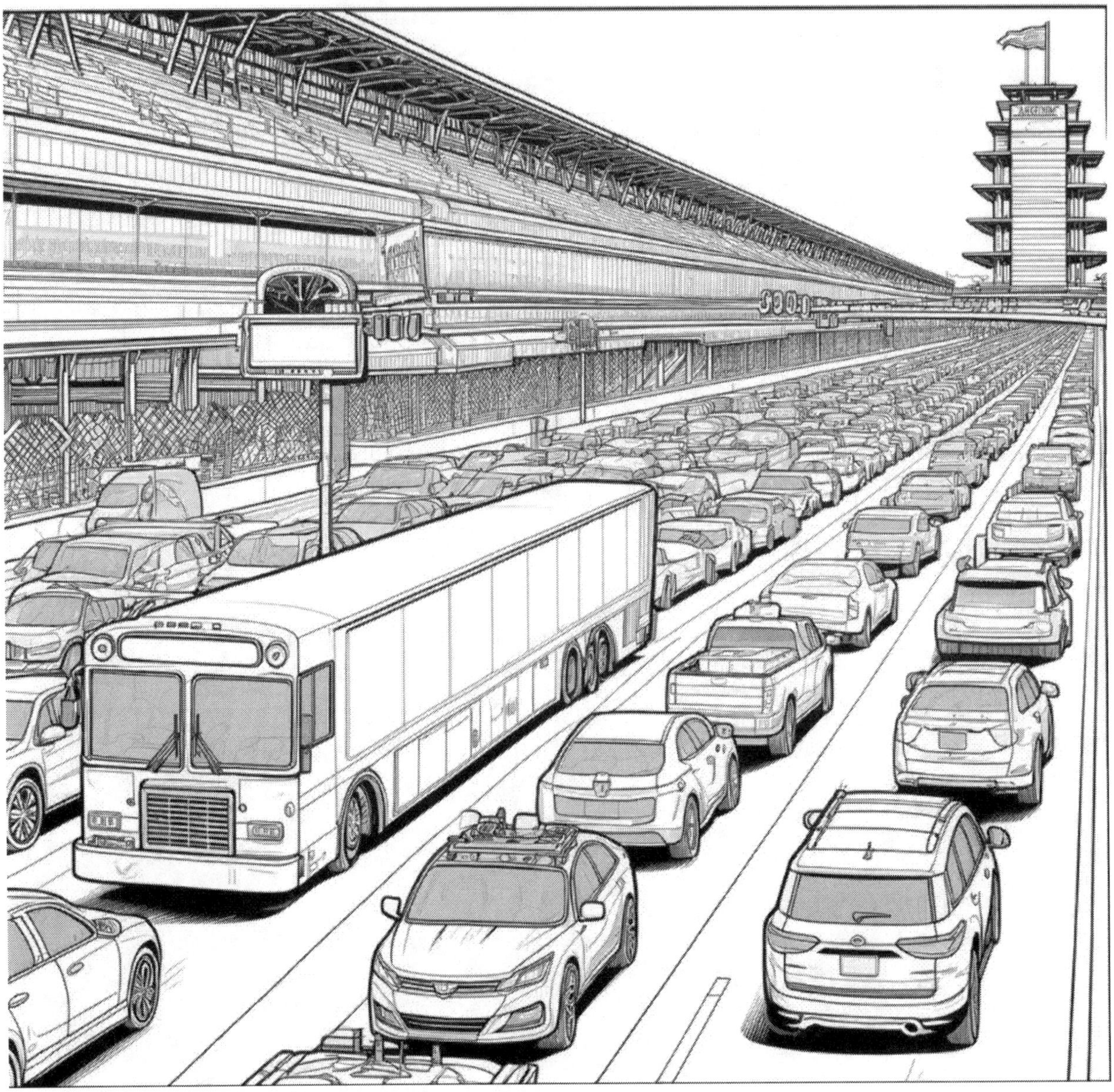

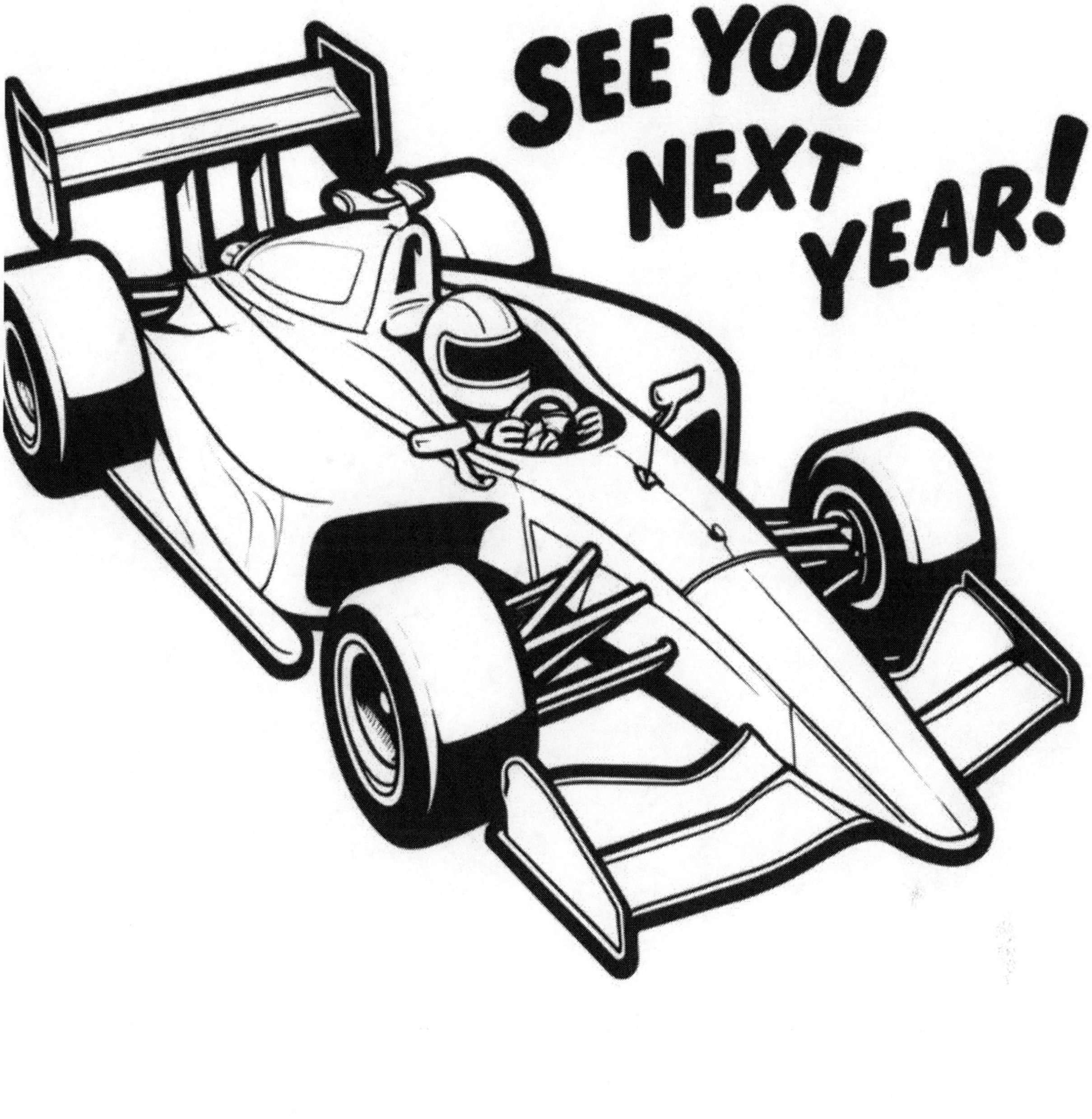
SEE YOU
NEXT
YEAR!

Made in United States
Orlando, FL
04 December 2024

54968929R00019